THE GRACIOUS TABLE

THE GRACIOUS TABLE

THE ART
OF CREATING
A BEAUTIFUL
TABLE

MARGARET CASELTON

RIZZOLI
NEW YORK

FOR EMILY, WITH LOVE

First published in the United States of
America in 1996 by
Rizzoli International Publications, Inc.
300 Park Avenue South,
New York, NY 10010

First published in Great Britain
in 1996 by
George Weidenfeld & Nicolson Limited
The Orion Publishing Group

ISBN 0-8478-1949-3
LC 96-68513

Printed and bound in Italy

Designed by Nigel Soper

CONTENTS

INTRODUCTION

I have always loved tabletop things: china, knives, forks, spoons, and glasses. Yet my china cupboard boasts only one complete set of matching pieces — and those I inherited from my mother. I collect cutlery from street markets and buy innovative and unusual pieces from crafts galleries. My glass cupboard is a hodgepodge of different styles, from inexpensive but classic wineglasses — what the Victorians discreetly but accurately termed elegant economy — to a few pieces of Lalique, mingled in with colored glassware and Moroccan mint tea glasses. Wherever I go I come back with something for the table.

Table setting for me is not about abiding by strict rules of etiquette. It is about creating your own still life — having fun with a dash of color here, mixing crockery patterns there, and deciding on which tablecloth provides the best background color.

My method is to select several pieces and experiment with one place setting, then I add another element or change the color of a glass, place a flower, and stand back and squint as if at a painting.

I adore flowers and for me they are the crowning glory of the setting. They are good friends — there to help you out. They complete the effect, lend softness of texture and natural color and form. It is essential to work flowers in tandem with the menu to avoid unappetizing collisions of color.

I have tried to incorporate a visual example of plain white china into most settings. White china is an ideal basic set, as it can be used very effectively to complement or contrast with any color, even gold and silver for a grand occasion.

Essentially this is a collection of ideas, a coloring book of themes and collages, and a few menu suggestions. I have also included a section on international table settings for reference, but they are not intended as the last word. There are several excellent books on modern etiquette available with much more detailed advice.

The ideas presented in this book are meant to encourage experimentation and boldness with color combinations, and to inspire confidence in developing a personal style. The important thing is not to worry about overdoing it — a bit of exuberance adds to the jollity of the occasion.

Bon appétit and have fun.

BLUE AND WHITE

Blue and white china has been popular for more than 400 years. It originated in China, where cobalt blue was painted onto porcelain as decoration before glazing. Imported by the East India companies into Europe, "china" became so established in Holland that it is known as Delft, after the Dutch town that became the major European center for its production. Important Staffordshire potteries in England, particularly Spode, manufactured transfer-printed designs, making blue and white china in a myriad of patterns – many of them Chinese – available to everyone. Odd pieces of these sets still exist and look very effective when grouped together. Such pieces may be easily picked up at antique fairs and markets, and larger sets might be found at auction houses. Collecting is an interesting hobby and valuable pieces sometimes turn up unexpectedly. Blue and white patterns are still in production, such as the traditional Willow, Spode's Blue Italian (which has been in continuous production since 1816), Geranium, Tower pattern, Asiatic Pheasant, and the elegant Blue Flowers by Royal Copenhagen. A good idea is to mix your collected blue and white china and, depending on the occasion, set it against a white or patterned blue cloth with a bunch of seasonal flowers.

FRENCH
BISTRO

This is a friendly, informal setting for lunch which is simple and fresh. Your choice of table setting will convey the mood of the occasion before the guests even sit down. A cheerful café style is achieved with a basic theme of blues and white, juxtaposed with checks and stripes. China and flatware are simple, utilitarian, and dishwasher-proof. Each setting is contained and uncluttered. The key to simplicity is a carefully considered use of color, pattern, and texture, built layer upon layer. Complete the look with equally simple accessories and details such as the checked napkin used as a focal point and a salad bowl potted with small daisies.

LEFT *Informal table
settings call for informal
flowers such as daisies –
in a dainty bunch or a
generous bowl.*

A pretty Victorian silver cruet set provides the necessary condiments and spices. Items you may have stored away in cupboards can be put to good use, serving a visual and functional purpose. This little set could be used equally well at a formal dinner, and here it injects a touch of elegance which offsets the "chunky" tableware.

A careful combination of detail sets the mood. The basic theme of blue and white creates a lively, informal atmosphere when set against a background of blue table linen in checks and stripes. An informal lunch means light but nourishing food. Here broiled goat cheese on bruschetta is served on a bed of lamb's lettuce and chopped walnuts, dressed with extra virgin olive oil.

Café-style china and glasses need to be offset by lighter elements such as country flowers.

Saturation and density of color can be achieved by the juxtaposition of different tones and patterns. Bring together mismatched linen, kitchen china, flatware, glasses – all in the chosen base colors – and place them together. A variety of napkins – such as one striped, one checked, one plain – looks cheerful.

Informal settings are often used in bistros. The knife and fork are placed together and set on a napkin to one side of the plate or on the plate.

Create a country atmosphere by using a homely container for flowers. Milk pitchers, enamel pitchers, or even jam jars filled with buttercups, dandelions, or common meadow flowers look charming. (Make sure they are plentiful and not a protected species before you pick them.) Tablecloths should be equally simple and can be cotton gingham, striped, or plain. Start a collection or make them from colorful dress or upholstery fabrics.

LEFT *Bread can be placed directly on the table in French café style.*

ASIATIC PHEASANT

A collection of Asiatic Pheasant, which was first produced in Victorian times, forms the basis of a special late-spring setting. The blue and white theme is enhanced by the soft pink and green of the full-blown peonies. As the china is not a complete set, we introduced floral-decorated coffee cups to complement the peonies. Table linen is fresh, starched, and white, with subtle floral embroidery. The original Asiatic Pheasant had a soft blue pattern, and became fashionable in the 1840s. The popularity of the pattern led to its being reproduced in the 1980s, and these modern versions can still be found, although the blue glaze may be somewhat darker than that found on the originals.

RIGHT *Simple glassware is best for lunch. Embellished glassware may look fussy, but pale pink or pale blue glasses would be effective.*

LEFT *Set on the table are the elements of a late-spring lunch party setting. The color theme consists of pink, blue, and white.*

RIGHT *Detail of china and flatware for one setting, showing the Asiatic Pheasant pattern.*

RIGHT *Stacked plates –
old and new – in the
popular Asiatic Pheasant
design. The soft blue
glaze lends a delicacy
that can be enhanced by
the juxtaposition of other
soft colors.*

The Asiatic

Pheasant pattern

has been popular

since the 1840s,

and old and new

pieces may still

be found. This

collection has been

put together over

more than 20 years.

Attention to detail is important, including the harmony of the color scheme, the texture and design of the linen, and the style of the flatware.

FAR LEFT *Some of these napkins are new and some are from antique shows or flea markets. All of them would be suitable for use in this setting.*

LEFT *It is important to establish a balanced composition of items of different height on the table – flowers, glasses, salt cellar and pepper shaker in this case.*

Flowers bring the setting to life and add a softness of texture. Buy flowers such as peonies and roses two days before you need them and let them open out.

BELOW *An example of the revived Asiatic Pheasant patterned china, which is currently in production. The blue glaze may have a darker hue than original pieces.*

One simple place setting in Asiatic Pheasant. All items, whether old or new, are linked by the 19th-century pattern and style.

A subtle floral theme links several elements such as the table linen, coffee-cup pattern, and peonies. Such detail is not always immediately noticeable but supports the harmony of the whole.

HARLEQUIN
BLUE

Spode blue-and-white-patterned plates from the Georgian Plate Collection, with different tones of blue underglaze and overlaying patterns, make an attractive table display. The blue-handled knives can easily be found at flea markets or antique shows. The "bishop's miter" napkin fold adds to the general embellishment; folding instructions are on page 138.

LEFT *A detail of the
china showing Spode's
Botanical, which was
introduced in 1826 in
response to a growing
interest in botany.*

ABOVE *Richly
embellished hock and
wine glasses echo the
blue and white theme.*

25 BLUE

AND

WHITE

A collection of old and new blue-and-white-patterned china is set out for a formal supper party on a summer's evening. On the table are two centerpieces for summer or winter: use both if you wish. If flowers are to be left on the table, they should be low so that guests can easily talk across the table. However, the generosity and height of this bunch creates a focus and a talking point. Flowers may also be cut to an equal length and one placed on each plate – some can last up to an hour in this way. Flowers brought by a guest could be used for this purpose. These would, of course, be removed before serving began.

RIGHT *A display of
the accessories used in
a blue and white
table setting.*

Use any blue and white dishes, a cake stand in white

china, blue- or white-handled knives — anything that

will enhance the theme. White embroidered table

linen and a pleasing bunch of white country flowers

and foliage bring life to the setting.

LEFT AND BELOW
This stack of blue and
white plates was
collected over 10 years.
Red pears displayed on a
Royal Copenhagen cake
stand create a pleasing
centerpiece and add
height.

Many patterns of blue and white china have

been in continuous production since the early

1800s. For this reason they are easy to find and

it should not take long to build up a small

collection.

CONTEMPORARY CLASSICS

There is such an enormous variety of tableware available to us, from so many parts of the world, that it is difficult sometimes to choose a service. Many contemporary examples will stand the test of time and become tomorrow's classics. A fine white dinner service will not date and looks effective on white table linen with simple flowers, or against a strong color. Most wedding china will be similar in style to our gold service (pages 30–31). The border color will differ, and can be taken as the theme. Notable also are Fornasetti's witty black and white and the colorful exuberance of Maryse Boxer's Rainbow china, left.

CLASSIC
GOLD
SERVICE

This elegant summer's evening setting for two or more uses a fine dinner service and crystal that are often included on wedding lists. Because it is simple and classic in design and style, the service can be used for different occasions. The key is the use of accessories to change the mood. Here a romantic setting is created by the unusual color of the full-blown roses and by keeping other colors warm, building upon the gold — the subtle edging of the glasses, the gold knot that decorates the flatware, the gold border of the napkins, and deep yellow beeswax candles.

CONTEMPORARY

CLASSICS

ABOVE *Place a gold-topped salt and pepper shaker set at each place setting. Alternatively, one set can be shared between two guests.*

LEFT *The silver flatware features a subtle gold knot in keeping with the color scheme.*

CONTEMPORARY

CLASSICS

This setting is predominantly gold and white. Any glassware should be clear, and accessories should be chosen carefully to harmonize with the color scheme. The gold and crystal sparkling in the warm glow of candlelight make for a romantic setting and create a comfortable, intimate atmosphere. Decanters, although not always necessary, add to the sense of occasion. Little bonbonnières may be used to hold candy, and taller dishes to show off fruits such as pink grapes, cherries, or peaches — anything to augment the color scheme and textures. A finger bowl filled with rose water and floating rose petals may be put on the table during the dessert course. Such details add to the splendor and romance of the occasion, ensuring the evening is special from beginning to end. Beeswax candles, the color of soft

parchment, burn quickly. Keep supplies handy, as they will need replacing. Roses in an unusual lilac color were bought two days earlier so they would "blow." The rose theme is repeated in the napkin rings.

LEFT *The accessories used in this setting reflect the gold and white color scheme — the crystal clarity of the glassware, the color of the roses, even the candy in the bonbonnière with their gold wrappers.*

RIGHT *If the first course is soup, the elements of a place setting are dinner plate, entrée plate, soup bowl, and bread-and-butter plate; a red-wine glass and a white-wine glass; dinner knife and fork, dessert spoon and fork, and soup spoon; coffee cup, saucer, and coffee spoon; and, of course, a generously sized napkin.*

The combination of gold, crystal, and rich, full-blown roses create an opulent setting. The choice of color of roses can change the setting from pretty to richly romantic. Tight-budded white roses with the gold make a pretty setting, while rich, velvety, dark red Nicole roses are emphatically romantic.

LEFT *From beginning to end everything must be perfect – even the coffee cups.*

LEFT *A detail of the placement of flatware. The napkin is placed on top of the soup bowl. The white-wine glass is usually placed to the right of the red.*

ABOVE AND RIGHT *Remove the thorns and tie a moss-green velvet ribbon onto the stem of a rose. Fold the napkin into a slim cylinder-shape, and tie the ribbon around it.*

BLACK AND WHITE

The combination of black and white creates an air of formality and cosmopolitan living. The juxtaposition of such dramatic opposites creates a stunning table setting. Fornasetti's designs based on optical effects and architectural perspective provide a lively variation on a theme. Many of the designs work together to produce a fascinating interplay of visual effects – witty and elegant at the same time. Black and white work well with the injection of a single strong color such as gold. Here we have used Fornasetti plates and gold-rimmed glasses set upon upholstery fabric that works effectively as a tablecloth.

LEFT *Fornasetti plates and gold-rimmed glassware set upon fabric printed with a classical design.*

BELOW *A simple theme of black and white may be easily achieved with white plates, a black tablecloth, and silver accessories.*

LEFT *The sun was a favorite motif of Fornasetti and it works as a simple, elegant design on this dinner service. With the current trend for East-meets-West cuisine, chopsticks can be useful and decorative.*

BELOW *Imaginary architecture is another favorite Fornasetti theme. Here architectural forms provide a decorative border on a classic dinner service. On dinner plates a white center with a decorative rim is often preferred for food presentation.*

Gold and silver accessories, bringing luster and sparkle, are the perfect foil for the black and white in the Fornasetti table setting. Vases are simple and flowers neat and budded. The cloth – Renaissance Collage by the English team Timney Fowler – forms the perfect backdrop with its vivid shapes of color.

*LEFT This wall plate
with its classical design
can also be used in the
dinner service, especially
against a cloth of roman
coins on a black
background.*

*RIGHT Serve black
and white food if you
are a purist. Squid-ink
spaghetti is served here
with sour cream and
caviar.*

*Fornasetti created no less than 500 versions of
the same woman's face. These plates are
precious but captivating and add humor to the
mood of the table setting. There are many
variations on the theme of black and white,
each one different from the last. It can be
interesting to keep a photographic record of
each setting.*

CONTEMPORARY COLORS

A combination of rainbow colors and unusual shapes in this unique dinner service designed by Maryse Boxer ensures a richly patterned setting that can be varied according to occasion and season. Below, the juxtaposition of strong colors and sympathetic curves creates a dramatic, modern place setting.

The jewel-like quality of bright glassware and
plastic-handled flatware brings a saturation of
color to the overall effect of the table setting. The
mixture of colored napkins, china, flowers, and
glassware has an almost kaleidoscopic effect;
patterns change with the progression of courses.
Gerber daisies are ideal flowers as their shape
and color are as emphatic as their surroundings.

LEFT *Lively
combinations of color
and shapes from Maryse
Boxer's collection of
rainbow-colored
ceramics and tableware.*

CONTEMPORARY

CLASSICS

RIGHT *A detail of a coffee cup. Each course of the meal will effect a kaleidoscopic change in the color scheme.*

A place setting in a single yellow color tone with petal-shaped plates creates a strong block of color and looks effective next to the same setting in a different primary color. The combined textures of china, flatware, and napkin also contribute to the overall effect. The soft pleated napkin can be knotted, folded, or tucked inside a glass.

The right choice of food is both necessary and fun when using bright-colored ceramics or glass dishes. Salads, fruits — such as pears poached in red wine, below — sorbets, and most summer foods look delicious in these settings.

A combination of colored, hand-blown glass dishes and colored wineglasses are placed for the dessert course. Make use of the bright hues of summer fruits to build up color contrasts on the table.

A collection of primary colors or a mixture of primary and secondary colors — such as green or orange — will always create a dramatic table-scape. Increase the amount of contrasting color or a color you are short of with flowers and fruits of that color.

CONTEMPORARY

CLASSICS

This jumble of ceramics, flatware, and glassware in a myriad of shapes and colors demonstrates an effective blend of hues. Colors should be carefully selected so that the table setting does not jar. For example, the introduction of black, stone, or beige would not work here. Use paint cards to experiment with color before you begin a collection. Unless you plan to dazzle, a white tablecloth is a good background. This cloth is made of white organdy inset with tiny Indian-style mirrors, each bordered with different-colored silk.

RIGHT *A rainbow of color in flatware, glassware, and napkins suggests a kaleidoscope of combinations that will create a dramatic tabletop.*

TOP *A three-tier setting of heart-shaped plates set off by a sugar stick is perfect for a Valentine's Day supper.*

ABOVE *This place setting combines square and curved shapes in orange with red-handled cutlery. The knotted napkin nestles inside the bowl but drapes over each side and the flatware.*

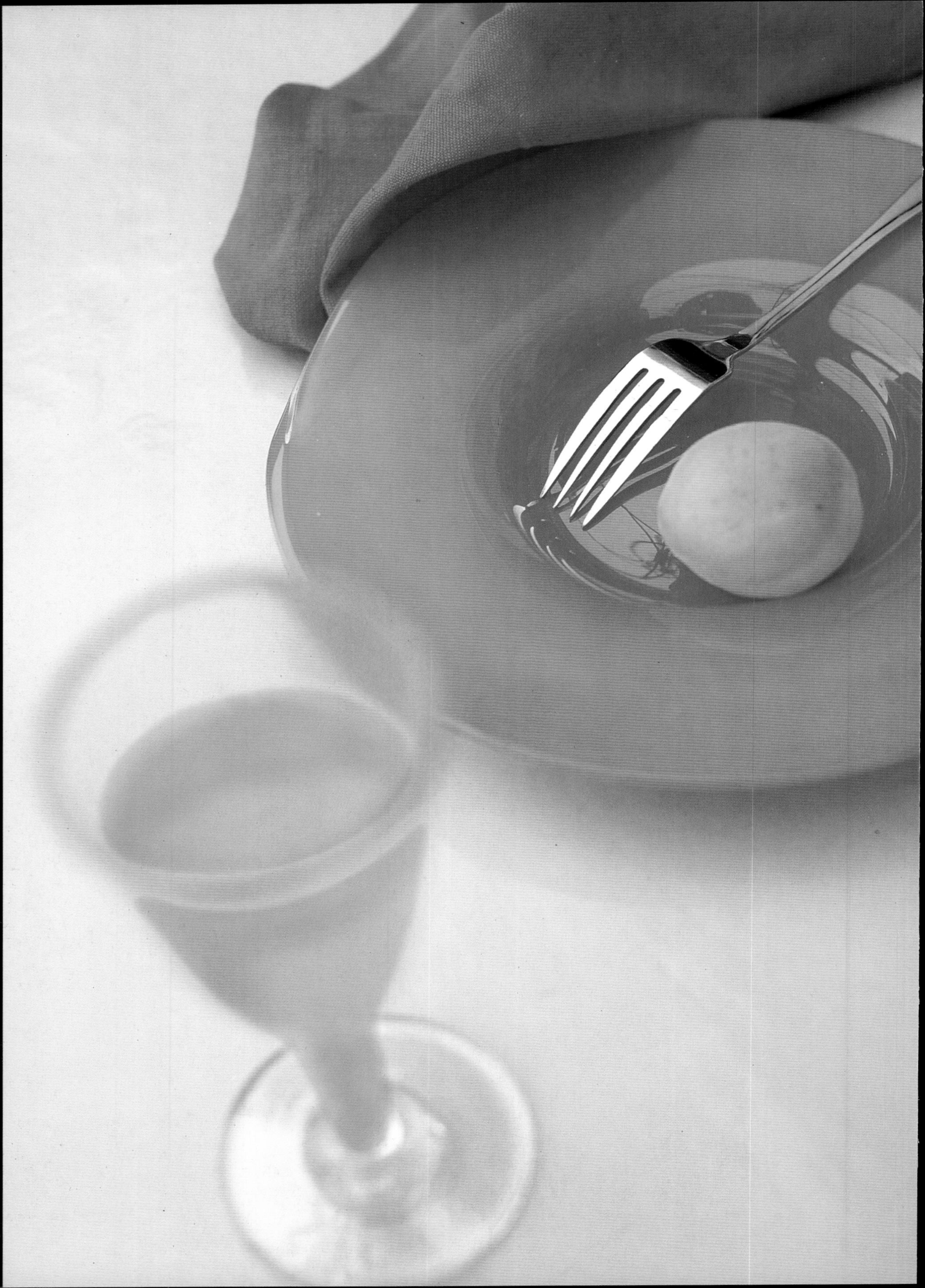

The individuality of hand-blown glass makes a definitive statement when used on the table or for display. Designs are often remarkable and a slight irregularity of shape makes a piece both charming and distinctive. You can commission your own glassware to a particular design or color. It is not difficult to find unusual contemporary glass at competitive prices. A large individual serving or display plate or a set of colored glasses will enhance any dinner table. Again, effective color combinations can almost achieve the quality of a still life.

Use the juxtaposition of colors to dramatic effect – limes or lemons against a bright-blue glass dish and orange Gerber daisies in a pale turquoise vase.

INFLUENCES FROM AFAR

We have always taken inspiration from other cultures, adapting their patterns, pottery, and precious metals to our own use. There are so many restaurants offering ethnic food and such a variety of imported ingredients that it is easy to experiment with exotic dishes. Enhancing the meal by providing an appropriate setting adds to the sense of occasion. So many fine tabletop items are imported from the Far East, Indonesia, the Mediterranean, Scandinavia, and many other regions that we are spoiled with choices. Collections from your favorite countries can be built up when you travel, which is great fun. Tablecloths made from colorful or exotic fabrics provide an effective background and offer more choice than traditional table linen. Lighting also creates atmosphere; a Mediterranean theme benefits from sunshine, while Moroccan and northern African settings look good with candlelit lanterns. Nordic wooden candelabra are charming, as are small Chinese table lanterns. Each table setting should reflect the influence of the chosen menu and the occasion.

CHINESE
STYLE

Chinese food is very popular and many Westerners are now adept at eating with chopsticks. Chinese markets are a rich source of traditional tableware and ready-prepared foodstuffs. The poppy is a perfect flower for the table and injects color into the setting.

LEFT *Tableware from Chinatown is set upon a remnant of shantung with red chopsticks and vibrant poppies.*

RIGHT *A traditionally shaped yellow Chinese teapot, cup, and saucer set upon a teacloth appliquéd with bamboo and lanterns.*

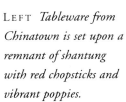

There is a Chinatown in many large cities, where tableware, chopsticks, and cooking implements are readily available. The traditional colors, patterns, and symbols all have particular meanings. The theme of the design of this tableware is prosperity, longevity, and happiness.

Tea is usually served with the meal. A small drinking cup is provided as well as a bowl, spoon, plate, and chopsticks. Chopsticks are placed on a chopstick rest. The spoon has a flat bottom so it may be set down without spilling the contents. Individual bowls are used for rice.

RIGHT *These are the eating implements and tableware for one place setting. The teapot is shared.*

ABOVE *Chinese sweet cakes.*

LEFT *Chinese chopsticks (far left) are usually fashioned into blunt ends, while Japanese chopsticks (center) have pointed ends. On the right is a child's pair of lacquered Japanese chopsticks.*

Depending on the Chinese pattern you choose, the color scheme can be enhanced by the addition of flowers such as poppies, peonies, or jasmine. This tablecloth is fashioned from a length of shantung, and the napkin is chosen for its color and silken quality. However, napkins are not used in China nor in Chinese restaurants; hot towels are provided for face and hands.

MOROCCO BOUND

An abundance of decorated Moroccan pottery, Fes and Safi bowls, relish dishes, brass coffee-pots and tin teapots, colored mint tea glasses, tagine and couscous dishes, and brass plates heaped with typical Moroccan produce all work together to create a richly exotic setting for a delicious North African menu. In the background a wooden screen is positioned so as to dapple sunlight onto the table and seclude the diners. Traditionally food is taken with the fingers of the right hand. A perfume bottle is used to sprinkle rose water onto the hands.

RIGHT *Various glazed bowls and plates are set against the geometric blue-and-yellow-patterned food dishes and Safi pots.*

LEFT *A tagine dish, with an open funnel for steam, is accompanied by a traditional brass coffeepot.*

BELOW *The elements of one place setting are set on table linen embroidered with traditional geometric patterns. Elegant minaret-shaped mint teapots are in common use throughout Morocco. Teapots and glasses are not expensive and may be purchased easily in Moroccan "souks" or specialist shops.*

Bring together pottery, pots, brass plates, and wooden spoons you have collected that share common themes — good color combinations, shapes, metalwork, Islamic patterns — and create an exotic table setting.

LEFT *The blue-glass and decorated silver perfume shaker in the center of the table is used to shake rose water into the hands after eating. The toothpicks are made from dried flowers.*

RIGHT *Spices in little dishes, olives, dates, and oranges can be used to conjure up a sensual Moroccan setting.*

Blue geometric-patterned pottery is common in Morocco and blends well with English dark-blue-glazed pottery. These dishes may effectively be used as serving or dessert dishes.

MINT TEA

Everyone stops for mint tea. This refreshing and invigorating beverage is de rigueur and easy to make. It is an excellent after-dinner drink and cleanses the palate. Right, a tray of mint tea is set out at the famous El Minzah hotel in Tangier.

1 *Make mint tea as follows: Put two heaping teaspoonfuls of green tea into a small teapot.*

2 *Add a good handful of fresh mint, and as many spoonfuls of sugar as you require (it is usual to drink this tea extremely sweet, with as many as 12 spoonfuls of sugar added to the pot).*

3 *Pour on the boiling water.*

4 *Serve the tea in glasses. A sprig or two of fresh mint in the glass adds to the flavor and appearance.*

1

2

3

4

MEDITERRANEAN

The ideal setting is outside. A large jar of sunflowers reminiscent of Van Gogh establishes the scene, along with a mélange of rustic terracotta pottery, traditional honey-glazed bowls, heavy ceramic pottery with a blue glaze and floral design, generously sized glasses, a gaily colored tablecloth, a few breadsticks, a jug or two of wine, cheese, salad, and good weather. Marigolds or any country flowers in season add to the overall color scheme. Line baskets with checked or brightly colored plain napkins and fill with rolls, tomatoes, or whole salad fruits. Then imagine yourself in the warm Mediterranean sun.

LEFT *A single place setting mixes terracotta from Portugal, a modern Quimper plate, and a traditional honey-glazed Provençal bowl. The tableware is set upon a length of turquoise Designers Guild fabric with large naive floral motifs.*

Select rustic tableware, café-style flatware, and colored glasses, and serve simple fare such as onion quiche and tomato and olive salad.

RIGHT *Place the knife and fork to the right of the place setting in an informal style. This is useful if space is tight.*

RIGHT *Various types of
Mediterranean pottery
are used in one place
setting.*

BELOW *Goat cheese
garnished with pink
peppercorns makes an
effective foil for a blue-
glazed plate.*

*The common theme among these settings is the
rustic feel of the ceramics, which, although
quite at odds in color and pattern, are similar
in texture and weight.*

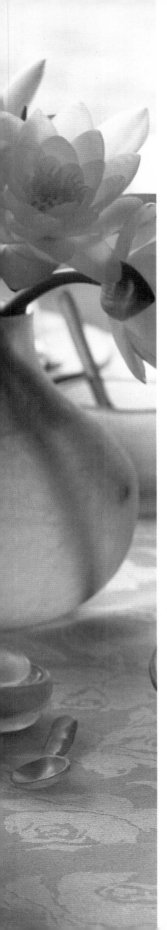

ALFRESCO

Eating outside is fun, whether it's a simple family barbecue on the patio, a summer lunch party, a wedding feast, or a picnic at an outdoor event. It can be formal or informal according to the occasion, but it is inevitably jolly and never fails to generate high spirits, even in the least likely guest. Everyone may bring a particular item of food and tableware, which usually ensures an element of surprise when the cloth is spread. Passionate picnickers have special hampers replete with china and flatware, ready-packed for impromptu opportunities on sunny days. Such a set can be quickly put together with simple colored plates, an assortment of glasses, cheerful gingham linen, and tin or enamel mugs. A fold-up table and chairs are useful, or take your cue from Manet and sit on the grass.

PICNIC TIME

A colorful gingham cloth catches the breeze at the beach. A galvanized bucket tied with a polka-dotted red hankie and weighted with pebbles serves as a wine cooler. Rough pieces of driftwood or sea-worn breakwaters make useful shelves for food baskets, and small mussel or cockle shells can be filled with seasonings such as salt. A tin milk pitcher, filled with red anemones, is anchored to the table with pebbles. The only problem remaining is to finish the meal before the tide comes in.

LEFT *A simple color scheme of red, white, and blue. A small stone keeps the gingham napkin on its plate.*

RIGHT *What better setting could there be for a picnic complete with champagne, flowers, and an improvised wine cooler.*

The key to a successful setting of this kind is to keep the color scheme simple and bright. Nothing should be too precious, as breakages are inevitable. The floor-length tablecoth is sewn from two lengths of gingham and has matching napkins. It is useful to have insect covers for food, especially in hot climates. Flowers may seem too much trouble to bring, but they provide a wonderful splash of color and create a sense of occasion.

LEFT *A detail of a single place setting in a red, white, and blue color scheme.*

ABOVE *A breakwater beam serves as a shelf for a basket of food. Line baskets with napkins to keep food clean and to continue the festive theme.*

LEFT *A white linen napkin embroidered with red checks especially for the picnic hamper.*

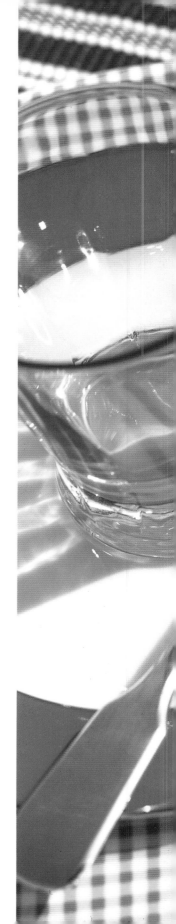

LEFT *Picnic food is usually eaten cold, and part of the joy is not to stand on ceremony but to eat certain things with your fingers. The pitcher is anchored by rocks in case the wind blows.*

RIGHT *This simple but effective setting mixes checks and stripes in red, white, and blue.*

Simple, colorful table linen and tableware work well on a picnic table or spread upon the ground. Combine checks, stripes, polka-dots, and solid colors in your chosen color scheme. Flowers, napkins, and bread baskets are the extra touches that make the event special.

Picnics are informal gatherings – you can either sit around a picnic table or spread a blanket or tablecloth on the ground. Finger foods are the order of the day, and a ripe Brie and tomatoes complement the color scheme.

SORBET COLORS

Eating outside is one of the joys that summer brings. Make the most of late sunsets, scented gardens, sea views, and the holiday atmosphere. Leisurely weekend lunches and summer suppers may be set up on a deck, terrace, patio, roof garden, balcony, on the lawn, or just by an open window. This atmosphere can be created or augmented by the evocative summer colors of a special dinner service. Here, pale frosted sorbet colors set the scene.

ABOVE *A tower of frosted resin sorbet dishes and matching spoon.*

RIGHT *A waterlily floats in each bowl, bringing symbols of summer to the table.*

Variations of frosted

pastel hues create a

delicate summer

table setting.

The delicate colors of this table setting create soft combinations that complement and reflect the pale blue ocean beyond. Build upon this delicacy with pale-colored or white flowers and a white or organza cloth and napkins. Flatware with glass or colored handles would work well. Each place setting here has its own condiment set, and this helps to cover the table with patterns of color.

Contrast the colors of the sorbet with the colors of the dishes.

RIGHT *The elements used in one table setting are, clockwise from the top: bowl, bread-and-butter plate and butter knife, water and wine glass, sorbet dish and spoon, napkin and ring, and dinner plate with spoon and fork.*

BELOW *The summer menu should suit the setting. Here a ripe peach makes a pleasing contrast set against frosted blue.*

Glass and similar materials (such as the frosted resin from Dinosaur Designs featured here) create a light, delicate setting. If the sun shines through them, colored shadow patterns appear on the table, which adds to the general effect. Waterlilies are particularly attractive floating in each bowl, but other large-headed flowers in bright colors would serve the same purpose.

SPECIAL OCCASIONS

Throughout life there are ritual celebrations to mark special occasions – christenings, birthdays, engagements, weddings, and anniversaries. In all societies there are festivals and feasts associated with the progress of the seasons and the religious calendar – New Year's, Valentine's Day, Easter, Thanksgiving, and Christmas. Each occasion requires attention to detail and planning of the menu, seating arrangements, and table setting. Flowers are always an excellent addition and add wonderful splashes of color to the plainest dinner service. These occasions present an ideal opportunity to polish silver, delve deep into china cupboards, light candles, bring on the champagne, fill the house with flowers, and prepare to make merry.

BEGGARS' BANQUET

A celebratory banquet at home is an appealing idea but seldom happens because of the expense. Here is an idea for a "banquet on a shoestring" that requires minimal outlay but lots of energy, enthusiasm, and innovative ideas. White sheets are used as tablecloths and enamel pitchers and mugs as vases with basic white china and stainless steel flatware for the setting. Trestle tables and "opera" chairs can be rented from a catering company.

RIGHT *Utilitarian trestle table and gold-backed chairs are rented for a cheerful "banquet" at home.*

A simple, functional banquet setting can be easily and economically put together with basic tableware, flatware, and drinking glasses set off by generous bunches of eye-catching blue iris.

It is easier to get a lot of guests seated if a place card is put at each setting. Here they are placed inside the wineglasses as the atmosphere is informal. Place settings may be cramped, and carefully crossing flatware within the bowl creates some extra room. No bread plates are necessary; bread may be broken and left on the table. Napkins are folded and placed under each bowl. If the trestle tables are narrow, it may help to present food buffet-style on a sideboard to be carried back to their places by the diners. Large pitchers of flowers can be removed, leaving the shorter arrangements in mugs for color.

ABOVE *An effective crossed flatware arrangement for a cramped table setting.*

RIGHT *Simplicity of form, texture, and color is the key to this setting.*

The necessary accessories are sheets to use as tablecloths, enamel pitchers (obtainable from hardware stores), salt and pepper for two or three guests to share, and colorful flowers.

ABOVE *Wineglasses can be used for desserts such as sorbets or fruit compotes.*

RIGHT *One place setting in detail.*

Large, informal dinner parties need to run smoothly, and it is therefore best to serve food that does not have to be prepared at the last minute, requires minimal attention once it is cooked, and looks appetizing on a white plate. Puréed vegetable soups or mixed salads with varied ingredients – radicchio, green bell peppers, baby yellow tomatoes, sliced red onions, black olives – are ideal to start. This Warm Chicken Salad is also a perfect choice; serve it with a crisp white wine. Keep desserts simple and brightly colored to end on a cheery note – sorbets and ice creams are always crowd pleasers. Bright orange mango sorbet looks wonderful with fresh raspberries and sprigs of fresh mint leaves.

GRAND

BUFFET

LUNCH

Historically, a buffet meal was always laid out

on a sideboard (the French word for this piece

of furniture is still buffet*). Guests help*

themselves from the food offered and carry it to

the table or sit down with plates on their laps.

If you plan a buffet for many guests, a

spectacular central display in a hall or large

room creates a gathering place and a talking

point which helps put people at their ease.

Smaller displays echoing the main theme may

be set up off to the side and chairs placed in

small clusters around tables or in groups

around the room to encourage mingling.

A large still-life display is set on a trestle table with a Flemish tapestry as a backdrop for a grand buffet.

This display is unashamedly inspired by the great Dutch still-life painters Van Os and Van Huysum, and others such as Velázquez. Art books specializing in the genre, catalogs of exhibitions, and postcards are rich sources of ideas. Long before rooms were set aside especially for dining, meals were set upon trestles and boards covered with cloths, heavy draperies, leather, or carpets, as can be seen in the paintings. Here those textures are emulated with a bright blue damask and two Victorian chenille table covers. Three boxes are placed underneath the covers to create different heights for display (see picture on page 93).

The juxtaposition of fruits and other textures work well in this setting. For maximum effect, combine unlikely and evocative elements and make visual puns such as the mandarin oranges in the blue and white china bowl.

LEFT *Plates are piled up and knives and forks are wrapped in individual napkins folded tuxedo-style; instructions are on page 138.*

ABOVE *Artichokes, cabbage, and quails' eggs on a pewter plate are evocative of a still-life painting.*

The focal point of this still life is the spectacular display of flowers, fruit, and vegetables. The receptacle is a plastic pot placed inside a large terracotta plant pot. Three blocks of florist's foam are placed inside with water.

1

2

3

FLORAL DISPLAY:
1 *Find a postcard of a still life you wish to copy and make notes about its structure. Place the stems of foliage, berries, and trailing ivy into the florist's foam first, following your skeleton structure.*

2 *Place the flowers, vegetables, and fruit in position. Artichoke stems can be wedged straight in, while fruits such as pomegranates or pineapples need to be pierced with florist's wire which is then stuck into the foam.*

3 *Fill out the naturally occurring holes with the remaining flowers, referring constantly to your inspirational painting.*

Flower stems are pierced into the foam and unwieldy fruits such as pineapples are threaded with thick florist's wire and held in position in the same way. In many paintings butterflies, small birds, or a snail can be seen. Models of such creatures could be added to the display.

*This detail of the
arrangement shows,
among other things,
parrot tulips, an
artichoke, a pineapple,
berries, lilies, red
ranunculus, and
delphiniums.*

BYZANTIUM

This lavishly adorned tableware – created by Peter Crisp – features slumped glass bowls and plates, silk-screened with various ornamental patterns in 22-carat gold, indigo, and green. These embellished plates and bowls are objects of art in themselves. The combination of gold and glass is startling and can be enhanced by candlelight to evoke romantic mood. The silverware, known as the Crisp design, was created and crafted by Lyndsey Davey especially to complement the tableware. Gardenias bring a heavy fragrance to the table.

LEFT *A polished refectory table set with this unique glassware and silverware. Individual place mats allow the grain and beauty of the wood to enhance the opulence of this setting and reflect the glow of candlelight. Gardenias bring their own unique fragrance.*

ABOVE *Gold upon gold – in glass or as a border on china – makes a rich table setting.*

ABOVE *Combine old and new with this Victorian silver and blue-glass salt and pepper set.*

ABOVE RIGHT *A single place setting for a three-course meal, including soup. The soup spoons are fashioned in the French style, with an oval bowl and pointed tip.*

Accessories for a dinner party based upon the grand theme of gold, glass, silver, and creamy-whites. Clockwise from the left are decanters and glass candle holders sparkling by candlelight, a candelabra and parchment-colored beeswax candles, creamy, scented gardenias and silver napkin rings.

As always, the menu should be planned with the setting in mind. The pale green of the cold asparagus soup goes well with the gold patterns on the dishes. Rich dark chocolate cake and a generous helping of cream suits gold as does the liquid gold of a good dessert wine.

Gold and silver go together. Left, an effective setting for a special occasion can be achieved with gold-rimmed china plates and silver flatware and accessories. The gardenia adds a finishing touch. Right, the requirements for one place setting. Note the large soup spoon at the bottom of the picture.

LEFT *Turn breakfast into a special occasion with an ornate eggcup and matching spoon set with mock pearls.*

RIGHT *This silver napkin ring features the guest's name.*

CHRISTMAS DAY

Christmas offers an excellent opportunity to create a festive table setting. It is the one occasion for which many families reserve special tablecloths, centerpieces, and napkins. The table is usually laden with candles, small gifts, and decorative objects. Traditional color schemes are green, red, and white. Red is always warm and welcoming. However, this table setting is inspired by the colors of Christmas roses and mistletoe. Warmth emanates from firelight and candles. A collection of white plates is a must for every china cupboard, as it can be combined with any color. Silk damask is used as a tablecloth and the chargers are tin cooking plates.

LEFT *Posies of
Christmas roses,
mistletoe, ivy, and
rosemary arranged in
green glass dessert dishes
create a light, refreshing
centerpiece at each place
setting.*

BELOW *Frosty themes
of green, silver, and
white for a Christmas
setting.*

*Typical accessories for a
Christmas setting
include tree ornaments,
miniature English
Christmas crackers, and
candles in appropriate
colors. Build up the
collection of colors,
adding gold for glitter,
and varying the shades
of green.*

The elements of one table setting. The dessert dish holds the Christmas posy.

This Christmas setting does not require a large investment; the elements may be collected together at relatively little expense. Green recycled glassware, pictured here, is now widely available, and the tin dishes used as chargers are easily found in hardware stores. These dishes can be effectively "pewterized" by baking them in a hot oven for half an hour. White or green napkins are equally effective, or a symbol of Christmas, such as a sprig of mistletoe, could be embroidered onto one corner. Decorate napkins with Christmas greens and berries.

1 For napkin decoration you will need a pair of wire cutters, florist's wire, a piece of ivy, and a sprig of mistletoe.

2 Twist florist's wire around the napkin and weave ivy over and under it. Secure the ends under the wire at the back.

3 Tuck mistletoe or berries under the wire to secure. Warning: ivy and mistletoe are poisonous and should not used for small children's napkins.

You will need a vase, clippers, and sprigs of choisya, ivy, mistletoe, freesia, Christmas roses, and rosemary.

Fill the dish with water. Place four pieces of choisya around the rim, then put four pieces of ivy in between.

Place bunches of rosemary between the choisya and ivy. Add two sprigs of mistletoe at four equal points.

Add four white Christmas roses and four white freesia, spacing them equally. Jasmine or other greenery with feathery leaves can be used to fill out the posy.

A posy bowl at each

place setting

establishes an

intimate and

welcoming

atmosphere and

creates the

impression of

attention to detail.

CANDLELIT SUPPER FOR TWO

This supper is intended for a romantic occasion – an anniversary, Valentine's Day, or a special celebration. The color scheme is gold and silver, with cream and white roses, which are scattered on shelves and tucked into each napkin. If you prefer traditional red roses, another color of tablecloth such as dusky pink would be suitable. The room is lit with slow-burning candles.

LEFT *The setting for a candlelit supper for two using a color scheme of gold, silver, cream, and white.*

ABOVE *A romantic heart-shaped candle holder – the perfect symbol of Valentine's Day.*

ABOVE *A collection of white, parchment, and barley-twist candles and holders. Don't forget to include a candle snuffer.*

RIGHT *A single place setting in Minton's Riverton service. A single creamy rose tucked inside the silver napkin ring adds to the decorative effect. A crescent-shape salad plate is placed to the left of the setting.*

A romantic supper for two at home has to be planned well and this may be difficult if the occasion is to be a surprise. As there will only be two of you, the less last-minute cooking the better. A cold hors d'œuvre such as oysters and a cold dessert are recommended, plus a simple main course such as baked salmon fillet.

BELOW *A novel and very personal idea for dessert would be a miniature frosted chocolate sponge cake decorated with white roses.*

RIGHT *Silver and gold accessories are used and set upon a "tablecloth" of handmade silk-screened fabric by Carolyn Quartermaine. Also suitable would be white damask or white linen, embroidered with gold thread.*

FLORIBUNDA

F *lowers are not only wonderful used fresh as table decorations, but are frequently the inspiration behind the design of dinner and tea services. Tablecloths, napkins, and tea cozies are often woven or embroidered with floral motifs; even flatware handles are sometimes embossed with flowers. Flowers are a simple and appealing theme to use as the basis of a table setting, which can be subtle and monotonal or extravagant and wildly colorful. Here rose heads are woven into garden chairs, and petals are cast, like confetti, over the terrace. A pretty coffee set on a white lace-bordered tablecloth helps to set a captivating afternoon scene.*

TEA AND ROSES

This color scheme is based on soft tones. The juxtaposition of Regency stripes, pink roses in two shades, green frosted glass, and a silver teapot and cake stand, all set upon a delicate embroidered organza tablecloth (over plain pink fabric which shows through), creates a soft, fresh setting.

FLORIBUNDA

FAR LEFT *Tea with scones, clotted cream, and strawberry jam.*

LEFT *In the pink for afternoon tea. Even the cakes complement the color scheme.*

FLORIBUNDA

Cut rose stems and plunge them immediately into water. If you wish them to open quickly, plunge them into warm water, with an aspirin to make them last longer. Buy or pick roses a few days beforehand if you want them to open and create a generous, almost full-blown, display.

1

2

1 *Sew tiny ribbon rosebuds onto a white tablecloth for a rosy effect. These little silk or satin decorations, which are frequently used in dressmaking, are available in many delicate colors. They create a busy background against which plain white plates can look striking.*

2 *Place a white cloth on the table you intend to decorate. Work out where each place setting will be, then sew the buds around the edges of the cloth and in the center.*

A cake stand is de rigueur at afternoon tea and enhances the display by offsetting and balancing the height of the flowers. Sandwich fillings of cucumber and smoked salmon match the color scheme.

FLORIBUNDA

Only a few pieces of this tea service remain, but a rosy patchwork effect is created by combining these with a contemporary silver teapot and creamer and fresh roses. Echo the rose theme in the posy, and make a rosebud-chain napkin ring. The pastry forks embossed with roses were a very lucky find.

Pieces of a pretty Victorian tea service with contemporary silver teapot and creamer.

Start a collection of floral-decorated plates with a color bias – such as a pink or pale blue background – and soon you will have a tea or dinner service. As flowers are such a popular theme, new or revived designs are frequently launched.

A selection of Limoges plates with floral patterns.

BREAKFAST
IN BED

Breakfast is usually such a hurried meal, if eaten at all, that most people consider it a real luxury to be brought breakfast in bed on the weekend. You will need a large, sturdy tray or a purpose-built tray on a folding stand. A flower theme and a colorful posy provide a cheerful morning greeting. Keep toast or rolls warm under cloths and a cozy on the teapot. Here the menu consists of grapefruit juice, a soft-boiled egg, toast, butter, home-made marmalade, and a pot of English Breakfast tea.

ABOVE *A large breakfast tray set with a colorful mixture of plates, pots, and cups featuring floral patterns.*

RIGHT *Pink ranunculus and grape hyacinths echo the flower arrangement depicted on the adjacent Dresden pitcher.*

DAYS OF WINE AND ROSES

Deep red roses set the tone for this elegant and substantial setting. The rose-patterned china echoes rose-embossed silverware, and the motif is repeated on the etched wineglasses and embroidered organza napkins. Everywhere the eye falls upon a rosy image. Every piece on the table is chosen for quality and elegance. Red and white rose petals scattered around create a festive atmosphere. Napkins are folded into a variation of the bishop's miter (see page 138 for instructions) and rosé wine is served.

RIGHT *Another variation on the theme of roses. Folded organza napkins lend an air of formality and define each place setting.*

OVERLEAF *The full table setting for a rose-themed formal dinner party.*

ABOVE *"Rose" silverware embossed with trailing roses, which also appear in delicate relief on the front and back of the spoon.*

APPENDIX

This Appendix includes a guide to international table settings and their variations, types of drinking glasses, and a visual glossary of the more common flatware pieces. It also offers ideas for napkin folding and place cards. The Appendix is intended not as the definitive word on etiquette but merely as a guide.

TABLE SETTINGS

1

ENGLISH FORMAL

The accepted procedure for laying a table is knives on the right and forks on the left. Soup spoons are placed on the outside right of knives and dessert spoons on the inside right. Sometimes the dessert spoon and fork are laid horizontally above the plate (see page 130). If in doubt, work from the outside inward, according to the order of courses. Sometimes a smaller, additional knife is placed on the bread plate or on the outside right of the setting. The bread plate is to the left of the forks.

1. BREAD-AND-BUTTER PLATE (SIDE PLATE)
2. NAPKIN IN A SIMPLE FOLD
3. TABLE OR DINNER FORK
4. DESSERT FORK
5. PLACE CARD

6. DINNER PLATE
7. FROM LEFT TO RIGHT, WATER GLASS, RED-WINE GLASS, AND WHITE-WINE GLASS
8. DESSERT SPOON
9. TABLE OR DINNER KNIFE
10. SOUP SPOON

2

SETTING FOR A CROWDED TABLE

If space around the dinner table is cramped, the bread-and-butter plate may be dispensed with and the napkin placed upon the dinner plate. The dessert spoon and fork are laid horizontally above the setting with the fork tines pointing toward the knife (right) and the spoon bowl toward the fork (left). If other eating implements are necessary, they can accompany their courses.

1. TABLE FORK	4. DESSERT FORK	7. WHITE-WINE GLASS
2. DINNER PLATE	5. DESSERT SPOON	8. TABLE KNIFE
3. NAPKIN	6. RED-WINE GLASS	9. SOUP SPOON

3

AMERICAN FORMAL

In an American setting the bread plate is set above the forks. If a butter knife is provided, it may be laid to the side of or above the bread plate. Both knife and fork are used to cut food, but the fork may be transferred to the right hand for eating.

1. NAPKIN
2. FIRST-COURSE FISH FORK
3. DINNER FORK
4. DESSERT FORK
5. BREAD-AND-BUTTER PLATE
6. DINNER PLATE

7. WATER GLASS
8. RED-WINE GLASS
9. WHITE-WINE GLASS
10. DESSERT SPOON
11. DINNER KNIFE
12. FISH KNIFE

4

FRENCH FORMAL

In a traditional setting, forks and spoons lie face down (originally to show the family crest). Sometimes knives are rested upon a porte-couteau (knife rest). Soup spoons are oval with a pointed end, except for consommé. Butter is never served with bread, so butter knives are not required. However, both a knife and fork are used to eat cheese, which is served after the main course (with the same red wine as the main course) and before dessert.

1. DINNER FORK
2. DESSERT FORK
3. DINNER PLATE
4. NAPKIN
5. SALT AND PEPPER SET
6. WATER GLASS

7. RED-WINE GLASS
8. WHITE-WINE GLASS
9. DESSERT SPOON
10. DINNER KNIFE
11. CONSOMMÉ SPOON
12. PORTE-COUTEAU

5

ITALIAN FORMAL

A formal Italian table setting depends upon the order in which the food is to be served, and whether there is pasta, fish, or soup first. If in doubt, work from the outside in, or wait for your host to select his or her implements before you begin. In this setting the fork on the far right is for risotto (first course), which is to be followed by fish and then meat.

1. FISH FORK
2. DINNER FORK (MAIN COURSE)
3. SALT AND PEPPER SET
4. DINNER PLATE
5. NAPKIN

6. RED-WINE GLASS
7. WHITE-WINE GLASS
8. DINNER KNIFE
9. FISH KNIFE
10. PASTA OR RISOTTO FORK

6

CHINESE FORMAL

The popularity of Chinese food has encouraged Westerners to use chopsticks. However, it is considerate to offer a spoon and fork as well to guests who may not have mastered the art. Rice is served into bowls by the host and people serve themselves the rest of the food from central bowls, but not using their chopsticks. It is not polite to "fish around" in the serving dish or attempt to cut food. If a morsel of food is too large it should be separated from other items and eaten on its own. The flat-bottomed spoon is used for soup or more slippery food.

1. TEACUP
2. BOWL AND SAUCER
3. TEAPOT
4. DINNER PLATE
5. SOUP SPOON
6. CHOPSTICKS
7. CHOPSTICK REST
8. LOW BAMBOO TABLE

GLASSES

7

FOR EVERY OCCASION

1	2	3	4	5	6	7	8	9

A good supply of red- and white-wine glasses together with tall and short glasses for mineral waters, soft drinks, and spirits is usually sufficient for a dinner party. Goblets or tumblers (whichever look more attractive with the setting) are suitable for mineral water. Glasses are grouped on the right of the setting above the blade of the longest knife. The usual procedure is to place the first-course glass nearest the diner. For example, the small white-wine glass that accompanies the first course (which may be fish) is placed on the outside right. If other glasses are required, they can accompany the course for which they are intended, especially if space is short.

1. GOBLET
2. CHAMPAGNE FLUTE
3. LARGE WINE (RED)
4. WINE (WHITE)
5. SHERRY
6. LIQUEUR
7. HIGHBALL GLASS
8. OLD-FASHIONED GLASS
9. BRANDY

FLATWARE

8

FOR EVERY PURPOSE

The Victorians invented
an eating implement for
every possible occasion.
Its particular function
was often to prevent the
fingers from touching
food. The Victorians are
responsible for fish
knives and forks, for
example, which have
been in continuous use
for more than 100 years
(but were considered
vulgar in certain
circles). If you enjoy
collecting silver, the
chances are most of the
decorative utensils you
find will be Victorian.
There are a variety of
soup spoons for different
soups, as well as jam,
tea, coffee, trifle, caviar,

1   2   3   4   5   6   7

1   2   3   4   5   6   7   8   9   10

1   2   3   4   5   6   7   8   9   10

and egg spoons. There are snail and pastry forks, and forks for every seafood imaginable. Originally, one knife (which the diner carried on his person) was used with bread as a "pusher". Individual forks began to be used in the 17th century. Early forks had two tines. "Silver" was used to describe eating utensils, for obvious reasons, but "flatware" is now the accepted term in the United States, "cutlery" in Britain.

KNIVES

1. TABLE OR DINNER KNIFE
2. STEAK KNIFE (WITH SERRATED EDGE)
3. CAVIAR KNIFE (WITH HORN BLADE)
4. TEA KNIFE
5. DESSERT KNIFE
6. FISH KNIFE
7. BUTTER KNIFE

FORKS

1. TABLE OR DINNER FORK
2. EARLY FORK WITH THREE TINES
3. STEAK FORK
4. FISH FORK
5. DESSERT FORK
6. FRUIT FORK
7. TEA FORK
8. PASTRY FORK
9. SNAIL FORK
10. OYSTER FORK

SPOONS

1. SERVING SPOON
2. DESSERT SPOON
3. ENGLISH SOUP SPOON
4. TRIFLE SPOON
5. ICE-CREAM SPOON
6. FRUIT SPOON
7. GRAPEFRUIT SPOON
8. TEASPOON
9. COFFEE SPOON
10. DEMITASSE COFFEE SPOON

TABLE NAPKINS

9

THE ART OF FOLDING

Fashions in the folding of napkins come and go. In the 17th century it was considered an art, and at Versailles napkins were folded into many shapes, including boats, chickens with eggs, and peacocks. It was a breach of etiquette to demolish these, so fresh napkins were supplied for use during the meal. Emily Post in the 1920s declared "fancy foldings are not in good taste," but today folded napkins, appropriate to the occasion are decorative.

TUXEDO FOLD

BISHOP'S MITER

JAPANESE FOLD

PEACOCK'S TAIL

PLACE CARDS

10

THE ART

OF

LABELING

If there are more than a few guests it simplifies seating arrangements to put place card at each setting. For a formal dinner, small fancy place card holders, such as the miniature silver pears above left, can be found at many good tableware stores. Another novel idea is to tie a place card to the stem of a piece of real or carved fruit. This works well at wedding receptions, with golden fruit and heart-shaped place cards. Or lay a flower tied with a velvet ribbon and the place card on a dinner plate.

MENU SUGGESTIONS

The following are guidelines for meals that would be appropriate for a selection of the themes found in this book. The dishes are all very basic and they have been chosen with the style of the setting and ease of preparation in mind, but there are a few basic principles that apply to all.

Like the table settings, the appearance of the food is important. When choosing a menu, consider the visual appeal of the food and strive for harmony with the setting, and remember to consider taste as well. White rice on a white plate with white fish in a white sauce (however delicious) would have the appearance of a convalescent meal. Conversely, a colorful fruit salad would lose its luster if served on a plate with conflicting color or pattern.

Be sure to choose a menu that is appropriate for the occasion, and when in doubt it is always best to err on the side of simplicity. If you attempt to overdo it, your guests will probably sense that things have been done to impress and this will not put anyone at ease. The best plan is to choose simple, elegant dishes that are not too fussy.

BLUE AND WHITE

FRENCH BISTRO MENU

The feeling is easy-going and the food should be chosen to match. Serve with carafes of lightly chilled beaujolais.

PÂTÉ, CORNICHONS AND CRUSTY BREAD

ROAST CHICKEN WITH GRATIN DAUPHINOIS

GREEN SALAD WITH VINAIGRETTE DRESSING

APPLE TART

HARLEQUIN BLUE MENU

The busy patterns of the setting call for classic dishes that will not further complicate the table.

ASPARAGUS WITH MELTED BUTTER AND GRATED PARMESAN

ROAST BEEF WITH BABY POTATOES

BROILED TOMATO HALVES, TOPPED WITH CRUSHED GARLIC AND MIXED FRESH HERBS

MIXED FRESH BERRIES WITH SWEETENED CRÈME FRAÎCHE

CONTEMPORARY
CLASSICS

CLASSIC GOLD SERVICE MENU

These dishes are the height of refined elegance and the romantic setting calls for an intimate, aphrodisiac menu.

PROSCUITTO AND MELON

MIXED STEAMED SEAFOOD: LOBSTER TAILS, SCALLOPS, MUSSELS AND SHRIMP

FRENCH CHEESE PLATTER

MUSCAT DE BEAUMES DE VENISE AND ALMOND BISCOTTI

BLACK AND WHITE MENU

This is a very classy menu with sophisticated flavors. An alternative entree would be oysters on the half shell.

SQUID INK PASTA WITH CRÈME FRAÎCHE

BAKED COD WITH ROAST GARLIC AND MASHED POTATOES, GARNISHED WITH CAVIAR

WHITE CHOCOLATE MOUSSE, SPRINKLED WITH GRATED BITTER CHOCOLATE

ESPRESSO

CONTEMPORARY COLORS MENU

Sharp, perky flavors to put on brightly colored plates – just be sure that colors harmonize.

BORSCHT

SALMON WITH MIXED STEAMED VEGETABLES (GREEN AND YELLOW SUMMER SQUASH, ZUCCHINI, RED BELL PEPPERS AND CARROTS)

KEY LIME PIE

INFLUENCES FROM
AFAR

MOROCCO BOUND MENU

This is a good menu for a large party as the main course can be made a day in advance. If blood oranges are in season, use them in the dessert salad.

AN ASSORTMENT OF GREEN, BLACK AND
PURPLE OLIVES

LAMB TAGINE WITH COUSCOUS

FRESH ORANGE SLICES, SPRINKLED WITH
ROSEWATER AND GARNISHED WITH FRESH
CHOPPED MINT

DATES AND MINT TEA

MEDITERRANEAN
MENU

This menu has a distinct Franco-Italian feel but any of the other Mediterranean cuisines (Spanish, Greek and Middle Eastern) are just as suitable and easy to preapre.

BRUSCHETTA WITH SUN-DRIED TOMATOES
AND PESTO

SALAD NIÇOISE MADE WITH GRILLED TUNA
STEAKS

APRICOT TART

ALFRESCO

SORBET COLORS
MENU

Transparent rice noodles look stunning on colored opaque plates.

WATERCRESS SOUP

STIR-FRIED VEGETABLES ON A BED OF RICE
VERMICELLI NOODLES

TRIO OF GRANITAS: LEMON, CANTELOUPE
AND CHERRY

SPECIAL OCCASIONS

BEGGARS BANQUET MENU

In keeping with the theme, the food should be easy to prepare, inexpensive and sure to please everyone.

BASIL AND TOMATO SALAD

———

CHICKEN CASSEROLE WITH RICE

———

FRESH FRUIT PIE

BYZANTIUM MENU

An assortment of Greek or Turkish dishes from a deli would complement the byzantine mood.

ASSORTED OLIVES, STUFFED VINE LEAVES, TABBOLUEH, HUMMOUS AND PITA BREAD

———

GRILLED LAMB AND CHICKEN KABOBS

———

BAKLAVA

———

TURKISH COFFEE AND ARAK

FLORIBUNDA

BREAKFAST IN BED MENU

Along with cheery floral-patterned china, this is the perfect menu to brighten up a cold, dull winter's morning.

FRENCH TOAST MADE WITH BRIOCHE

———

CHERRY AND PLUM COMPOTE INFUSED WITH A VANILLA POD

———

CINNAMON COFFEE

———

SUNDAY PAPERS

DAYS OF WINE AND ROSES MENU

Choose a fine French Bandol rosé to complement the setting and the following dishes will be a perfect match.

BROILED GOAT CHEESE ON A BED OF VINAIGRETTE-DRESSED SALAD LEAVES

———

PAN-SEARED TUNA STEAKS WITH RATATOUILLE

———

STRAWBERRY ICE CREAM WITH CRYSTALIZED ROSE PETALS

INDEX